MASTERING
SELF-DISCIPLINE

*How to develop self-control to achieve
your goals successfully*

TABLE OF CONTENTS

INTRODUCTION

Are you ready to apply self-discipline and take your life to the next level? Do you have the motivation and dedication to get started? The first step is to understand what it takes to develop self-discipline.

Despite the numerous goals we set out to reach, life can be full of unexpected roadblocks. These obstacles can hinder our ability to make positive life advances and prevent us from getting ahead. Finding ways around or over these barriers can seem daunting, but getting creative and looking for solutions outside the box can empower us to continue. Developing a plan, scheduling time wisely, and adjusting when needed may help one find success in challenging situations. Recognizing that there are many paths to take before reaching our final destination allows us the resilience and determination required to achieve personal accomplishments.

In this tumultuous world of ours, one of the greatest gifts we possess is self-control. Mastering our reactions and our emotions can be a great benefit in all aspects of life. The way to acquire such an ability is through deliberate practice. It's not easy, but by making an effort, we give ourselves room to grow. As challenging as each moment may be, if we are determined to override our impulses with thoughtful intentions, we allow for greater opportunities instead of providing negative reinforcement for lackadaisical techniques. With time and hard work, anyone can learn how to overcome these obstacles and create a secure foundation of self-control.

This guide will provide the necessary skills and knowledge to become a master of self-discipline. Through a combination of understanding, practice, and application, this guide will help those seeking to gain control over their lives and increase one's self-awareness. Chapters will focus on the basics of self-discipline, how to overcome challenges, the habits and techniques of building self-control, and how to use it to reach your goals. With this newfound knowledge, you can adjust to life with self-control and develop a sense of pride in your accomplishments.

The journey toward mastering self-discipline is not easy, but the rewards it will bring are worth the effort. Committing to self-growth and personal development can unlock the door to a new, more rewarding lifestyle. So, take the first step and discover all that self-discipline offers. Good luck on your journey!

CHAPTER 1:
THE BASICS OF SELF-DISCIPLINE

Self-discipline is critical to success in any field, from schoolwork to sports and even career goals. It involves setting clear objectives and then pushing ourselves to attain them despite the obstacles and other influences that would typically sidetrack us. Developing self-discipline requires focusing on reaching our goals and consistently paying attention to our actions until they are complete. It can be learned over time with practice, patience, and persistence, but it creates good habits that help us stay organized and motivate us to achieve our objectives.

With self-discipline, you can create the environment and mental strength needed to reach any desired outcome, requiring less energy in a shorter amount of time overall. This chapter will discuss self-discipline, why it's important, the psychology behind it, the benefits of using self-control, and the consequences of not using it. By the end, you should better understand how self-discipline can be used to reach goals and why it is essential for success.

What Is Self-Discipline?

Self-discipline is about taking ownership of your behavior, setting expectations for yourself, and following through with them, regardless of how challenging it may be. It's the difference between telling yourself, "Yes, I can," instead of "No, I can't." Whether resisting unhealthy late-night snacks or slogging through a troublesome task, exercising self-discipline builds character and gives us the power to take control of our lives. It's also very empowering as we realise that we can impact our life's destiny by controlling our actions. Self-discipline isn't easy, but leading productive lives and reaching our aspirations are essential.

The Psychology behind Self-Discipline

Our ability to exercise self-discipline is vitally important in our daily lives, yet it may often be overlooked. According to the psychology behind self-discipline, this trait relies on an individual's ability to set and maintain manageable goals while simultaneously resisting temptations or distractions. When developing self-discipline skills, it is beneficial to recognize personal weaknesses and strengths and tailor a plan accordingly.

For instance, one might create realistic rewards for tasks completed, such as taking a 15-minute break after completing work assignments. Similarly, practicing the "two-minute rule" of getting started on challenging tasks immediately when feeling unmotivated is crucial. Through perseverance and mindfulness of unhealthy habits, it is possible to craft personal strategies that enable us to build up our self-discipline and reach the goals we have set for ourselves.

The Benefits of Self-Control

Self-control is indeed a superpower. It can be defined as a person's ability to control behavior and emotions, especially in challenging situations. It takes effort to exercise self-control, but its benefits are indisputable. Those who practice self-control tend to be better communicators and problem solvers, more proactive when reaching their goals, and better able to stay emotionally balanced when faced with intense situations. Self-control also gives us the capacity for

4

delayed gratification, essentially an ability to enjoy greater rewards (and save money) by patiently working towards our goals instead of impulsively going after immediate results that often dissipate quickly.

A. Focus and Discipline

Self-control and discipline are essential to the pursuit of any meaningful goal. It takes great strength of character to stick with objectives even when things get tough, or results are not coming as quickly as we'd like. Doing so requires a balance between self-reflection and action. Without discipline, it is easy to become distracted by other pursuits or give up in the face of difficulty. With focus and discipline, however, comes profound rewards, both intangible, such as heightened confidence and improved time management skills, and tangible such as increased success in our careers or personal lives. The benefits can be pretty remarkable for those willing to commit to self-control.

B. Stress Reduction

Practicing self-control is a great way to reduce stress and improve mental well-being. Self-control plays an essential role in managing emotions, decision-making, and relationships. It helps us recognise bad habits, resist temptation, battle procrastination, and make healthier choices. By learning to take control, we can gain the confidence to create positive changes in our life so that we may better manage our stress and reach our goals quickly. Reducing stress through developing self-control techniques leads to increased enthusiasm and happiness as well as improved health, both physical and mental.

C. Improved Self-Awareness

Improved self-awareness can help people develop several beneficial qualities that increase their chances of having a successful future. One key area of improvement is the benefit of increased self-control. People who take the time to pause and reflect on their behavior can gain insight into how they manage their impulses and make the most positive decisions for themselves. Having this greater understanding of one's thoughts, feelings, and behaviors allows people to take greater ownership over their lives by having more focus and purpose with every action they take. You can strengthen your ability to practice self-control for your long-term success, health, and well-being through improved self-awareness.

D .Increased Productivity

Having self-control has a plethora of benefits, especially when it comes to productivity. It allows us to break down seemingly insurmountable tasks into smaller achievable goals and gives us the discipline to ensure they are completed. By utilising self-control to focus on one task at a time, we can avoid distractions that interrupt our workflow and, as a result, stay productive for extended periods. Self-control also heightens our ability to prioritise tasks and make well-informed decisions about what needs to be done first, saving us time in the long run and maximising our output effectively. These elements can positively impact our ability to complete projects faster and more accurately than ever.

E. Improved Health

Most of us have heard the phrase 'moderation in all things.' This proverb emphasises the importance of self-control to properly balance out negative and positive impacts on our bodies and daily activities. Improved health can be one of the ultimate benefits of this discipline. Self-control can help keep unhealthy temptations at bay, such as eating that third slice of cake or smoking one last cigarette and replacing these choices with healthier ones like fruits and vegetables or going for a pleasant walk instead. Self-control can be challenging at times, but it is worth the effort. stress levels, improve moods, and improve overall being. With improved health thanks to increased s can all look forward to longer, healthier lives.

The Negative Effects of Not Using Self-Control

Self-control is an essential skill that requires you to manage your thoughts, feelings, and actions. When it is not used, the effects can be quite damaging. Ignoring one's own goals and succumbing to distractions can lead to a life of feeling overwhelmed and confused. Habits like procrastination, overthinking, and substance abuse can develop as a way of avoiding responsibilities. Not exercising self-control may also weaken relationships with family, friends, and co-workers and have adverse physical health outcomes like unhealthy eating habits and lack of exercise. Therefore, cultivating the power of self-control is vital to leading a positive life full of purpose.

6/22/23 STOPPED

A. Poor Decision-Making

Poor decision-making can have detrimental consequences on our lives, yet too often, we don't exercise self-control and find ourselves in difficult situations. When faced with the possibility of making a wrong decision, our first reaction is to think about what we want right now rather than consider our future well-being. We may reason that simply choosing the option that appears most exciting at the time is harmless enough.

Unfortunately, even seemingly innocent decisions made without proper consideration for the long term can eventually result in much more severe problems down the road. For example, shopping sprees or bouts of binge drinking can quickly evolve from a momentary lapse in judgment into a terrible financial strain or severe health issues. Without taking responsibility for our actions by ensuring reful thought is put into each decision, negative repercussions are inevitable.

B. Stress and Anxiety

Stress and anxiety are two leading mental health issues affecting people worldwide. Living in an unpredictable environment, it can be difficult to handle situations with self-control. Unfortunately, not attempting to manage reactions to life's challenges can lead to long-term physical and mental problems. When we become overwhelmed by our stress levels or anxiety sets in, it's often because we haven't tried to take control of ourselves and focus on solutions. Staying aware of our thoughts and feelings is essential, as avoiding these issues can result in serious physical manifestations such as lack of sleep and increased risk for disease. Employing self-control is the first step in managing stress and anxiety and reducing their harmful effects.

C. Unfulfilled Goals

Not achieving goals can lead to an unpleasant feeling of disappointment. That disappointment often leads to blaming either ourselves or external factors. We create a damaging cycle of negative thinking by not taking responsibility for our lack of self-control, which could have helped us achieve our goals. Our self-criticism and pessimism shape our day-to-day mindset and impair our motivation to keep pushing forward toward success. Without self-control, we are doomed to continuously react from one emotion to another without any real constructive action in achieving our goals. In other words, it is through maintaining control that we actively participate in steering our lives in the direction we want them to go.

D. Low Self-Esteem

Low self-esteem can often be traced to a lack of self-control. When we cannot control ourselves, it's easy to get frustrated and discouraged. We may become overly critical of our behavior and believe we're undeserving or unworthy. Our sense of self-worth carries over into other aspects of our lives, negatively impacting decisions and eroding confidence. The insidious thing about low self-esteem is that it develops slowly and subtly, often without us realizing it, until it becomes an issue. Taking the time to practice self-control is an essential step towards preventing these feelings from taking hold in the first place, ultimately helping us avoid their adverse effects on our daily lives and long-term goals.

E. Health Issues

Health issues related to a lack of self-control can cause problems over time. Not only can this lead to an unhealthy lifestyle, but it can also create chronic conditions due to poor diet and lack of exercise. This can affect both physical and mental health. Negative thought patterns, anxiety, and depression can result from insufficient self-control to reign in unhealthy habits. A healthy lifestyle is essential for both physical and emotional well-being, which is why it's crucial to develop strategies for self-control to maintain optimal levels of both. Taking the time to ensure healthier living patterns will help mitigate potential future health issues down the road.

Key Takeaways

- Self-discipline is the practice of taking responsibility for our actions and behaviors.
- Stress and anxiety can be managed with self-control.
- Not achieving goals can lead to feelings of disappointment and low self-esteem.

- Health issues can be caused by a lack of self-control regarding diet and exercise.

- Self-control is essential to leading a healthy lifestyle, both physically and mentally.

Action Step

Develop strategies for self-control to maintain optimal levels of physical and emotional wellness. Write down these strategies in a journal and review them regularly to ensure that you stay on track. Start small, set achievable goals, and work your way up. Be patient with yourself as you move forward on your journey toward success. Celebrate even the smallest of achievements to keep yourself motivated.

Chapter Summary

Self-discipline is an essential part of life that must be cultivated to reach our goals, manage stress and anxiety, prevent negative thought patterns, and maintain physical and mental health. Self-control is the key to achieving our goals and maintaining an overall positive outlook on life. Taking the time to practice self-control and create healthy habits will help us be successful in whatever goals we set for ourselves. By developing a sense of self-discipline and actively monitoring our thoughts and feelings, we can break free from the cycle of disappointment and low self-esteem and achieve greater success.

CHAPTER 2:
OVERCOMING CHALLENGES TO DEVELOPING SELF-CONTROL

Self-control is one of those qualities that allow us to control our lives. It's an essential tool for helping us reach our goals and live more satisfying and fulfilled lives. Unfortunately, some aspects of life can prevent us from mastering this skill. Naturally occurring temptation and the urge to run away from responsibility generally make it difficult for many of us to stay on track by developing self-control. Managing these aspects is critical in improving our ability to regulate ourselves and ultimately learn to exert self-control in all facets of life.

This chapter will cover the various obstacles preventing people from developing self-control and how to overcome them. It will discuss procrastination, lack of motivation, distraction and how to move past them to master self-discipline. By understanding the challenges and knowing how to manage them, we can provide ourselves with the tools necessary to develop self-discipline. The following subsections will discuss the obstacles to developing self-control and strategies for overcoming them.

The Challenges of Developing Self-Control

Self-control can be a challenge for people of all ages since it takes much mental energy to avoid giving in to temptation. We learn over time and must practice on an ongoing basis to become better at controlling our choices and reactions. We need self-control when making healthy lifestyle changes, staying levelheaded during a stressful situation, or preventing ourselves from impulsively spending money. Through continuous effort, anyone can develop greater self-control. The key is to be patient with yourself and remember that positive habits take time to form. Strategies such as setting boundaries, recognizing triggers, journaling your thoughts and feelings, and avoiding situations with potential temptations can help you learn how to become more self-controlled.

A. Procrastination

Procrastination can be a difficult habit to manage effectively. For many, it stems from an inability to balance tasks adequately between short-term and long-term goals. The challenge of self-control revolves around the idea that by delaying the gratification of the momentary pleasure or reward, we can achieve more tremendous success in the longer term. To successfully break free from procrastination requires self-discipline and motivation. Implementing daily activities geared towards achieving goals can provide a focus for individuals struggling with procrastination. Focusing on meaningful goal setting is essential for developing the discipline to overcome procrastination regardless of how much we may want to give in to our temptations in the short term.

B. Lack of Motivation

Developing self-control is a difficult but necessary task. When motivation starts to waver, visualizing long-term goals can bring and maintain focus over the short run. Identifying distractions and limiting access to them can significantly aid in this process and tracking progress on different tasks and projects. Changing habits and behaviors that are no longer productive requires dedication and repeated practice. Enlisting the support of friends, family, or mentors who guide you in pursuing individual goals may be beneficial. Even when unmotivated, establishing small milestones can help push forward until momentum is achieved. Developing self-control takes persistence and may seem daunting at first, but it becomes more accessible and rewarding with consistent effort.

C. Distractions

Positive behavioral skills and intrinsic motivation require self-control. With it, even the most talented individuals can reach their highest potential. Distractions can be particularly detrimental in this regard. The temptation of multitasking is a constant challenge for many people, but if we are mindful of how distractions can disrupt our focus, we can learn to exert control and limit them. Self-regulation allows us to choose how we want to react when facing circumstances that demand our full attention and effort. With slight adjustments in mindset and lifestyle decisions, anyone has the opportunity to accomplish great feats despite the presence of distractions.

D. Social Pressure

Social pressure can be a major challenge when it comes to developing self-control. We are often more swayed by what others think or say than our own more profound convictions. We naturally want acceptance and approval from friends, family, and peers, which despite being important in life, can lead us to make decisions that aren't always the best for ourselves. It is crucial to balance pleasing those around us and making choices that truly reflect what we value or believe in.

13

To do this, having a solid understanding of our values and morals is essential as being able to courageously stand by them even if they are unpopular among friends or colleagues. Self-control comes initially through cultivating an awareness of one's thoughts and actions and then making intentional decisions. When making decisions under social pressure, self-control can be challenging to achieve. Yet the effort is undoubtedly worth it if you're hoping to attain balanced decision-making.

E. Impulsiveness

Impulsiveness can often be a challenge, especially when striving to develop self-control. Our innermost desires can sometimes blur the lines of reason and cause us to act impulsively on sudden urges that may have long-term consequences. It is possible, however, to assert control over these outbursts and live with more deliberation in your decisions by relying on sound judgment instead of short-term gratification. Effective coping strategies can help us stay above temptations and be prepared for situations where our impulses may take over. With resilience, we can learn how to respond responsibly even in moments of intense emotion, thereby gaining greater mastery over our actions.

Strategies for Overcoming Challenges

Everyone faces challenges throughout life, and to be successful, it is vital to have strategies for overcoming those obstacles. No one should feel like they must overcome every single challenge alone. Talking with others may give you insight you wouldn't typically have seen. These combined strategies can help anyone turn frightening obstacles into victorious accomplishments!

A. Identifying Your Obstacles

Identifying and overcoming obstacles is an essential part of personal growth. Taking that first step and recognizing the roadblocks holding you back can be intimidating, but the rewards can be incredible. To get started, reflect and determine what stands explicitly in the way of your success. Determine why each obstacle remains and brainstorm ways to conquer it.

When it's time to take action, set realistic goals and revisit them often as checkpoints to record progress. Finally, ensure you are held accountable for achieving these goals with regular check-ins with friends or colleagues for positive reinforcement and honest feedback when needed. Identifying obstacles is a great way to create a plan for success and lasting change!

B. Setting Realistic Goals

Setting realistic goals can be a powerful tool for overcoming challenges and helping to reach your objectives. Having achievable targets helps motivate, as reaching each one is a psychological incentive for progress. Breaking down any significant challenges into smaller, more manageable chunks also helps to ensure that complex tasks don't seem insurmountable and makes it simpler to take a logical and practical approach to resolve the issue.

Reviewing the process at regular intervals allows for previously-set benchmarks to be reexamined, allowing you to adjust the plan according to any changing circumstances. With enough practice and persistence, setting realistic goals can help you stay focused and have incredible determination when confronting life's most significant challenges.

C. Developing a Plan of Action

Developing a plan of action to overcome any challenge can make it easier to achieve the desired outcome. Careful consideration should be given to any goal and the strategies necessary to reach it, as success often depends on how well the plan was laid out.

Identifying and allocating appropriate deadlines for each task required to achieve the goal is essential.

Having someone qualified and knowledgeable agree with each step is also helpful, as they could be an invaluable source of information, guidance, or support in times of difficulty. Taking this proactive approach to solving challenges can enable you to work through them quickly and efficiently, paving the way for future successes.

D. Using Positive Self-Talk

Positive self-talk is an invaluable tool for overcoming small and large life challenges, as research has consistently indicated that our thoughts shape our reality and determine how we interpret events. If we view ourselves positively and take control of our self-talk, we can better prepare ourselves to face the inevitable difficulties and roadblocks that life throws our way.

Positive self-talk gives us the confidence to proactively approach obstacles while reaffirming that whatever happens will be manageable and that we can make it through safely. Additionally, it can strengthen our inner dialogue, encouraging us to grow and learn from challenging experiences instead of being overwhelmed or demoralized by them. With positive self-talk as part of one's daily mindset practice, difficult times become an opportunity for growth rather than undesirable hardships.

E. Taking Time to Relax and Unwind

Taking time to relax and unwind is essential in overcoming the challenges that life throws your way. Slowing down can help to combat the feeling of being overwhelmed, allowing for better clarity and insight. Taking a break also allows you to take stock of your situation and think objectively about how to tackle complex problems. By redirecting focus away from your immediate worries and enjoying activities that bring peace, relaxation can help reframe how you think about the situation. Practicing regular relaxation techniques such as yoga and deep breathing exercises can promote mental well-being, helping you move forward with hope rather than fear.

F. Avoiding Self-Sabotage

One of the most vital strategies for overcoming challenges and avoiding self-sabotage is recognizing what triggers our negative thoughts and behaviors so that we can proactively work to oppose them. Focusing on identifying the source of a problem rather than becoming overwhelmed by it can help us develop a plan of action to find solutions. Additionally, understanding when our approach and mindset may be damaging our progress and leading us towards dangerous patterns of self-sabotage allows us to pause before we take action or alter course at the first sign of distress.

Embracing difficulty as part of life, rather than viewing failure and struggle as setbacks, can also provide valuable insight into how to push ourselves further without risking long-term negative consequences. This creates an effective strategy for conquering whatever challenges stand in your way while safeguarding your mental health and well-being from potential pitfalls.

Key Takeaways

When looking for the best way to tackle a challenge:

- Break down the problem into small parts. This allows you to identify underlying issues and work towards them little by little until they are solved.

- Look at the situation differently to see alternative or creative solutions when other methods are ineffective.

- Taking breaks can also help because pausing will allow time for new ideas and energy in tired minds if you feel overwhelmed or stuck.

- Finally, seeking out help when needed can make all the difference.

Action Step

Now that you're familiar with the various strategies for overcoming challenges, it's time to implement them. Please choose one of the tips above and implement it today to build the skills necessary to overcome obstacles and reach your goals. Remember to focus on small steps at first so they can be easily accomplished and become part of your daily routine.

Chapter Summary

Self-control is an essential life skill, and it can be difficult to develop without a certain level of strategy. The key to mastering self-control lies in recognizing and overcoming numerous obstacles, such as procrastination, lack of motivation, or fear of failure, which can stand between us and our goals. With practice, we can learn practical approaches for overcoming each issue, allowing us to build upon our successes as we move closer to achieving our objectives. By doing this, we will discover that self-control is within our reach.

CHAPTER 3:
HABITS AND TECHNIQUES FOR BUILDING SELF-CONTROL

Self-control is essential for achieving success in life and accomplishing our goals. It involves implementing strategies such as organization, discipline, and reflection on our actions. With self-control, we can manage stress more effectively. We're better able to focus on the task at hand, think before we act instead of impulsively responding, and stay on track with long-term objectives. Developing self-control also encourages us to form healthy habits such as eating nutritiously, exercising regularly, and getting adequate rest.

Good habits lead to good decision-making, which ultimately yields positive results that help propel people toward their goals. Self-control offers endless rewards when leveraged correctly. This chapter will discuss various techniques and habits that can be implemented to help build and master self-control. It will cover topics such as establishing routines, breaking long-term goals into smaller chunks, and setting achievable daily targets. By the end, you will have the tools and skills to help improve your self-control.

Establishing Routines

Establishing routines can be a worthwhile addition to your life. It takes dedication and patience, but your rewards will be well worth the effort. Routines simplify decision-making throughout the day and create structure, allowing for an easier way to focus on productivity and goals. They provide an anchor in our day-to-day lives that help us live more intentionally, making us feel calmer and find moments of stillness amidst all the chaos. Finding what routine works best for you may take trial and error, but stay dedicated and have consistency until you can form and maintain lasting habits.

A. Breaking Long-Term Goals into Smaller Chunks

Achieving long-term goals can be daunting, but the truth is that it does not have to be! By breaking big goals into smaller chunks and establishing good routines, you can make those goals seem much more manageable. Establishing good routines builds the foundation for success by creating a structure your life can build on. Each day is full of small achievable tasks that work together to help you reach your overall goal. Even when feeling overwhelmed with a difficult task, having a routine will enable you to focus on one action at a time until it is complete. With consistent dedication, you will soon look up and realize how far you have accomplished on your journey.

B. Setting Achievable Daily Targets

Setting achievable daily targets is a great way to establish healthy and productive routines. The trick is to make sure your tasks are manageable and realistic so that you don't become overwhelmed with the workload or set yourself up for disappointment. Focusing on small, incremental steps can help alleviate anxiety around taking on big projects. Additionally, mapping out a timeline of when each task will be completed is a handy exercise for practicing mindfulness while creating positive behaviors. Discipline, in its simplest form, is the decisions we make each day. Setting achievable daily targets can ultimately turn into good habits that reap the rewards even outside work.

C. Developing an Accountability System

Establishing good routines is critical to setting up an effective accountability system. Good practices help us stay on track by reinforcing positive behaviors and inhibiting the tendency to fall back into bad habits. To maximize an accountability system's effectiveness, be consistent in following through with routines that are established. This will develop confidence in the system and encourage one to engage in productive activities more often. Recognizing small accomplishments while striving for larger ones can also provide additional motivation as we strive to reach our overall goals. Ultimately, accountability systems can help us get closer to our objectives through consistent effort and vigilantly adhering to established routines.

D. Making Time for Self-Reflection

Regularly carving out time for self-reflection is a proven way to stay grounded and connect with the thoughts swirling in our minds. Establishing routines around setting time aside can help us stay mindful of our physical and mental well-being. By scheduling brief, dedicated moments every day or week devoted to self-reflection, we have a better opportunity to pay attention to our emotional needs and growth. It's like checking in with ourselves.

Routines are also powerful tool that helps create a positive mindset. The cumulative effect can be enormous by taking small daily steps, even if only five minutes. A reflection routine doesn't need to take place in any particular place. Since reflection is personal, it can be done anywhere that works for us. Whether it involves yoga, meditation, journaling, or something else, taking thoughtfully scheduled pauses for ourselves is just as critical as breathing!

E. Resisting Short-Term Urges

Establishing effective routines is a wise course of action to gain control of your life and better manage those urges to give in to the short term. Start by determining what you want to draw long-term success out of, and then create a plan of action that focuses on breaking up that goal into short habits. Complete one or two of these small habits daily to cultivate an overall sense of progress and stay focused on achieving your larger goal.

When implementing a new routine, creating healthy reminders can be beneficial in giving yourself that initial push, whether setting the alarm for yourself or enlisting someone who can encourage you when times get tough, having effective methods in place to help you remember why this routine is essential may make reaching your goals easier.

Implementing Self-Discipline Techniques

Developing self-discipline is vital if you want to achieve success in life. Self-discipline can help you stay focused, stave off procrastination, and prevent you from becoming overwhelmed by your goals. To get the most out of your efforts to develop self-discipline, you must choose techniques that suit your individual needs and lifestyle. Finding activities to boost determination and consistent practice of self-discipline techniques are critical components of success. Incorporating behaviors such as setting aside specific times dedicated to a discipline activity or task, being accountable to yourself and others, or tracking progress will all move you closer to implementing effective self-discipline techniques.

A. Visualization

Implementing self-discipline techniques for effective visualization can be difficult at first but can create positive change in our lives. One method is to find a quiet place and close your eyes, picturing what you're striving to achieve with its accomplishment in detail. Whether it's financial stability or a healthier lifestyle, envision yourself as if these desires have already been accomplished: what would that look like? Practicing this visualization once a day can help increase motivation and clarity. Focusing on the outcome lets us see what we must do to achieve those goals. Visualisation is essential to creating the life you want, finding discipline to stick with it can make all the difference.

B. Meditation

Practicing meditation can be an incredibly effective way to improve self-discipline. This simple yet powerful exercise helps us learn to stay focused on the present moment and use our energy wisely. Through meditating, we can develop the habit of being mindful in our daily lives, which requires a great deal of discipline. By turning our attention inwards, we can start identifying tendencies that sabotage our progress and find ways to replace them with positive habits. As we continue this practice, we become increasingly disciplined in how we use our time and energy, ultimately leading us closer to our desired outcomes.

C. Repetition

We've all heard the phrase 'practice makes perfect,' which certainly rings true, especially when implementing self-discipline techniques. Repetition of good habits is crucial in developing new routines and behaviors. Fortunately, there are many steps you can take to help reinforce your goals. By breaking down large tasks into achievable chunks, you'll be surprised at how swiftly you can achieve what once seemed impossible.

You can also set reminders or establish consequences for not completing these minor tasks. Once again, repetition is the secret! Use apps or time-tracking methods to structure your time and ensure you're on track with your daily goals. Implementing self-discipline may be challenging at first, but before long, it will become second nature.

D. Positive Reinforcement

Self-discipline techniques, goal setting, and regular positive behavior reinforcement are essential to implementing positive reinforcement successfully. Regularly assessing progress can also be incredibly useful for reinforcing positive behavior. By recognising progress, a person is incentivised to keep advancing. Additionally, continually introducing new challenges and skills will further energise and motivate someone to stay disciplined. If implemented correctly, positive reinforcements as a self-discipline technique can strengthen habits and ensure success in any endeavor.

E. Making Connections

To effectively implement self-discipline techniques, it is essential to connect actions and outcomes. That means we must learn to recognise the connection between how we act today and the future results of those actions. This enables us to prioritise to achieve our goals. These practice habits lead to success, delaying short-term gratification and being resilient to challenging situations. By understanding our patterns of behavior and holding ourselves accountable for them, we can take control of our one precious life and unlock its true potential.

F. Taking Action

When aiming to make a positive change in our lives, often the biggest challenge is finding the necessary motivation to implement it. Self-discipline provides us with the tools needed to strive toward our goals persistently. Various self-discipline techniques can be adapted to make it easier to take action. These may include setting and upholding deadlines, creating rewards for yourself when achieving desired behaviors or outcomes, and breaking tasks into manageable chunks. By consistently utilising these strategies, we can better combat any moments of procrastination and make gradual progress toward our chosen objectives. Taking action through self-discipline gives us a golden opportunity for personal growth and encourages us to expand our limits of what we deem possible.

G. Adaptability

Adaptability is a crucial trait to success in life and at work. One of the best ways to become more adaptable is by implementing self-discipline techniques. These involve focusing on personal goals, developing healthier habits, and being mindful of how our behavior affects others. Self-discipline also includes taking responsibility for mistakes and having the strength to persevere even when something gets difficult. By utilizing these techniques and understanding the benefits that come with them, you can increase your ability to be flexible, resilient, and adaptive. Adopting self-discipline will help you become the person you strive to be and succeed in any endeavor.

Key Takeaways

- Self-discipline is critical to achieving a sense of balance in our lives. It enables us to understand better and manage our time, priorities tasks, and plan for success.

- By consistently exercising self-discipline, we can recognize opportunities, set, and reach goals, gain confidence, and ultimately experience more favorable outcomes in our personal and professional worlds.

- Developing the muscle of self-discipline helps us stay on track no matter what distractions life throws at us.

Action Step

Now that you understand different self-discipline techniques and their importance, it's time to take action. Make a plan outlining how to use these strategies to help increase your self-discipline. Think about what areas of your life could benefit from extra focus and dedication, and start incorporating these techniques into your daily life. Set realistic, achievable goals and create a timeline to help you stay on track.

Accomplishment begins with committing ourselves to consistent action and making responsible decisions, requiring effort but rewarding us with attention to detail that leads to lasting results. In short, having self-discipline propels us towards reaching for bigger dreams in all areas of our lives, opening the door for growth with limitless potential.

Chapter Summary

This chapter discussed various techniques and habits for building self-discipline, such as establishing routines, breaking long-term goals into smaller chunks, and setting achievable daily targets. Additionally, the importance of taking action and being adaptable was highlighted to maximize growth potential. Self-discipline helps us stay on track, reach for bigger dreams, and realize our true potential.

CHAPTER 4:
APPLYING SELF-DISCIPLINE TO ACHIEVE YOUR GOALS

Unsurprisingly, many successful individuals credit their successes to goal setting. Setting goals provides a road map to direct efforts and determine progress, which can be incredibly motivating. When you have established clear objectives, they can help identify potential pitfalls while striving for success. Incorporating a plan of action to pursue your ambitions is paramount if you want to reap the rewards of your hard work. Goal setting is an essential strategy that allows us to achieve our dreams and reach unprecedented heights.

This chapter will focus on how to apply the concepts learned in the previous chapters to achieve our goals. We will discuss topics such as how to stay focused, prioritise tasks, and develop a growth mindset. Additionally, we will discuss the importance of practicing self-control to be successful when pursuing our goals. Self-discipline, when developed, can be a great asset in helping to reach our goals. By following these steps, you will be well on your way to achieving your ambitions!

Staying Focused

Staying focused and applying self-discipline is essential for achieving our goals. Whether getting through a strenuous workout routine or starting a new project, having the will to see it through can be a significant challenge. However, knowing how to use the right tools and create goals that are meaningful to us will help us stay on track. We should pause and reflect on our progress to determine which strategies are practical and modify our plans accordingly. By understanding what motivates us, we can assess if our tasks align with our values and desired outcomes, enabling us to tap into our internal resources with greater clarity and diligence. With that focus and motivation, anything is possible.

A. Setting Priorities

Staying focused on a task can take time and effort, especially when dealing with multiple responsibilities or sudden plan changes. Setting priorities and sticking to them is an essential tool for staying focused. This means prioritising activities according to importance, allotting separate time slots for each item on the list, and remaining firm in your decision to stay the course until it's completed. This mindset boosts productivity levels and clarifies competing tasks, allowing more complex projects to be approached methodically and confidently. Ultimately, relying on good organization instead of impromptu action will lead to greater focus which can result in tangible achievements and heightened successes over time.

B. Eliminating Distractions

Distractions can be a real enemy of focus and productivity. Whether it's an online rabbit hole or a sudden craving for snacks, distractions can quickly take us down the wrong path while trying to stay productive. To eliminate these obstacles, developing proper habits is vital. Constantly monitoring our focus, removing possible distractions before they occur, and having someone to hold us accountable can help us to remain focused on the tasks at hand. Additionally, taking regular breaks from work to reset and recharge helps our brains get back in the right frame of mind to stay focused when jumping back into position. By implementing these tactics and creating good practices for eliminating distractions, one can become their most productive self.

C. Developing a Growth Mindset

Two crucial skills are having a growth mindset and applying self-discipline to reach our goals. A growth mindset is an attitude of wanting to continuously learn and grow, while self-discipline helps us stick with our goals until we've accomplished what we set out to achieve. Working with these two skills creates a steadfast work ethic that can lead us to success. When facing challenges or setbacks in making progress towards your goals, focus on developing a growth mindset that will help you find creative solutions and take advantage of learning opportunities. Don't let fear of failure stop you from persisting. Use self-discipline to stay focused and motivated, and progress can be made! Adopting a 'never give up' mentality and using creative thinking combined with discipline is perfect for achieving your goals.

D. Taking Time to Reflect

Taking time to reflect is a vital part of keeping focused. When we're caught up in our busy, daily lives, it can be challenging to find the time to step back and check in with ourselves, but making a conscious effort to do this can make a huge difference. Taking a few moments, whether taking a break from work or walking at the end of the day, can help us gather our thoughts and remind ourselves what we are striving for. Taking time for self-reflection allows us to remember why we are doing what we are doing and gives us insight into what steps we can take to achieve our goals.

Regular reflection helps ensure that we stay on track, organised, and motivated in all areas of life.

Practicing Self-Control

Practicing self-control regularly is essential to leading a happy and healthy life. It helps build mental strength, as well as provides you with the ability to navigate difficult situations more. Self-control can be broken up into two main parts: emotion regulation and impulse control. The former requires one to recognise and reflect upon their emotions and channel them into positive thinking or action. Impulse control involves identifying when it's better not to take specific steps or partake in certain behaviors for your benefit. These key components provide invaluable coping tools for everyday challenges and struggle that everybody inevitably faces. Working hard to cultivate self-control can ultimately result in more productive use of time, healthier relationships with those around you, and improved overall quality of life.

A. Establishing New Habits

Establishing new habits can be difficult, especially if that habit requires self-control. Many of us know the feeling of starting a diet, exercising, or taking on another life change enthusiastically, only to find ourselves back in our old routines after a few days or weeks. To remain on track and successfully make positive changes to our lifestyle, it's critical to practice self-control. Self-control helps us stay consistent and do things we may not enjoy that are necessary for progress. It also gives us the power to adhere to routines even when faced with temptations that might otherwise divert us from our goals. With the determination to stick with it and the will to control our impulses, implementing new habits can become second nature.

B. Making Adjustments

Practicing self-control can be difficult, b but s off in the long run. Adjustments start with becoming aware of our actions and reactions, such as how we respond to stress or crave a particular food. Once we become conscious of this, we can start to make progress. We start to positively reframe our thoughts, being mindful of our emotions rather than suppressing them and shifting unhealthy habits into healthier ones. Small steady steps go a long way in building self-control which will help us lead happier lives. Changing how we think and act sets us on the path to better understanding ourselves and controlling our impulses. Acknowledging that making more conscious decisions leads to greater control of our lives is critical to building discipline.

C. Developing a Plan of Action

Developing a plan of action for practicing self-control can be a daunting task. Determine what you are trying to control, and assess how best to do it. Consider the goals you want to achieve ahead of time and make sure timelines are realistic. Set yourself up for success by developing positive reinforcement techniques that allow you to take small victories along the way. Regularly review your progress and discuss any barriers or challenges so they don't overtake your motivation and sense of loyalty to your plan of action. With consistent practice, dedication, and hard work, self-control can help you achieve whatever you set out to accomplish.

D. Tracking Progress

Achieving goals can be challenging, but tracking your progress is a great way to practice self-control and ensure you are focused on the task. It can help bring awareness to how much time and effort you put into each goal. Tracking progress also makes it easier to identify triggers when obstacles arise. For instance, if you start procrastinating with a particular goal, tracking progress will help monitor what could be causing this shift in focus. Learning about one's behavior and reactions helps build self-awareness, determine what works best for success, and refine self-regulation capabilities.

E. Celebrating Successes

Taking the time to celebrate successes is essential to achieving success and developing self-control. Taking a moment to recognize how far you have come will motivate you for your next step forward. It doesn't matter if that means congratulating yourself with a pat on the back or some small reward. Any action taken to show appreciation for your achievements will allow you to solidify a feeling of accomplishment. Recognizing your successes will be essential in developing self-control as you strive for more significant challenges and potential future achievements.

F. Learning from Failures

Everyone experiences failure. It comes with trying something and not having it become a success. Acknowledging that you have failed and moving on from it is crucial to learning from those failures. Choosing to continue down the same path, or even punishing yourself for failing, halts progress in the long run. Having self-control after failing means appreciating your mistakes for what they were and letting go of them when you're ready instead of clinging tightly to the guilt that comes with them. Self-control allows us to look our failures in the face, identify what went wrong and why, and figure out how to improve ourselves to have a healthier relationship with predictability in our pursuits. Learning from failures requires allowing yourself enough space for reflection without spiraling into self-blame, which requires self-control.

G. Staying Positive

Practicing self-control is one way to cultivate greater positivity within ourselves. Recognizing and responding mindfully to difficult thoughts and emotions is vital to self-control, enabling us to take more balanced actions and decisions. Taking the time to pause and reflect on the present moment can help us identify opportunities for responding to our internal states with less impulsivity, which can lead to more satisfying outcomes. Even if it sometimes feels challenging, staying positive by practicing good self-control is worth the effort. It will give us greater peace of mind, foster healthier relationships, and enable us to make better choices for ourselves in the long run.

Key Takeaways

- Staying focused, prioritizing tasks, and developing a growth mindset are essential to achieving one's goals.

- Tracking progress helps bring awareness to how much time and effort you put towards each goal and identify triggers when obstacles arise.

- Celebrating successes is essential in developing self-control as you strive for more significant challenges and potential future achievements.

- Learning from failures requires allowing yourself enough space for reflection without spiraling into self-blame, which requires self-control.

- Practicing self-control is one way to cultivate greater positivity by recognizing and responding mindfully to difficult thoughts and emotions.

Action Step

Track your progress to help you stay focused and on task towards achieving your goals. Take the time to recognize and celebrate successes, big and small. Reflect on failures without going into self-blame or punishing yourself for not succeeding. Practice self-control by responding mindfully to complex thoughts and emotions. Overall, stay positive!

Chapter Summary

Self-control is a tool that can help us achieve our goals and lead healthier, more satisfying lives. Practicing self-control, staying focused, prioritizing tasks, developing a growth mindset, tracking progress, celebrating successes, and learning from failures is crucial. Finally, staying positive and practicing good self-control is essential to keep our spirits up and make better choices for ourselves. By understanding the power of self-control, we can take greater control of our lives and make positive changes. Self-control can help direct your life in the direction of your goals. With the right mindset, determination, and commitment, you cannot limit what you can achieve.

CHAPTER 5: ADJUSTING TO LIFE WITH SELF-CONTROL

Self-discipline is a crucial element to achieving success and happiness in life. Although it takes vigilance to establish, the results can be gratifying. Developing good habits helps us build self-control, restrain our temptations, focus on our goals, and take responsibility for our decisions. Many successful people credit their accomplishments to the attribute of long-term self-control. They stay steadfast in their visions and objectives through determination, sustained motivation, and consistency. With enough dedication and commitment, it is possible to reap great rewards from this skill.

This chapter will cover how to adjust to life with self-control, including the importance of having a support system and self-care. It will also discuss how to maintain self-control over long-term periods and how to handle relapses. With these strategies, you can become a master of your destiny and break through the barriers preventing you from achieving success.

The Importance of a Support System

Establishing a solid support system is an essential step to achieving self-control. It provides reassurance on tough days, but having people in your life to fall back on can also give you the necessary tools and resources to live on your terms. Learning how to avoid bad habits, such as smoking or drinking too much, can be done with the help of those closest to us. Their unconditional love and care could help us shape our lives into something we feel proud of. We should be setting goals while also striving to create healthy relationships. This way, we can find the balance between relying on someone else and taking responsibility for our well-being. With a sound support system backing us up, learning to lead a meaningful life with self-control is possible.

A. Staying Connected

A supportive network of family and friends is incredibly important for overall well-being. They provide emotional reassurance, serve as a valuable source of advice, and can even help build self-confidence. While taking time to nurture these relationships is essential, we're all busy these days, so it can be challenging to stay connected. Thankfully, modern technology has given us ample opportunities to do just that. Although you may not meet up with your loved ones in person as often as you'd like, staying in touch takes a few clicks away. Strong relationships are the foundation stones of life's most profoundly meaningful moments.

B. Reaching Out for Help

We all have times when life is complicated and need extra help. Having a solid support system around you is essential to getting through tough times and can provide much-needed comfort and security. Whether it's a mental health crisis, an emotional setback, stress from school or work, or dealing with family drama, some people can be trusted to provide the guidance and advice needed to help make positive decisions. Reaching out for help, whether talking to friends or family for comfort or meeting with a professional for more specialized care, is a significant step in self-care that should never be underestimated. Building a reliable support system so that you can access their help whenever needed will enable us to cope better with any challenging situation.

C. Finding a Mentor

Having a mentor or support system is often an overlooked yet special tool for personal and professional growth. A mentor can be found in many forms, from family members to employers to colleagues. They offer guidance, provide resources, give advice, hold us accountable, and are available for questions about the current or next step in a process. When making difficult or uncharted ground choices, having access to people who have successfully navigated similar obstacles can make the difference between success and failure.

Mentors also provide honest reflections on our strengths and weaknesses, making them necessary agents of change. If you're looking for development or career advancement opportunities teaming up with a mentor can help open doors that are otherwise closed off without their assistance. The importance of having someone who encourages us to reach our potential cannot be overstated!

The Importance of Self-Care

Self-care is one of the most significant things you can do to improve your overall physical and mental well-being. When you practice self-care, you allow yourself to connect with your body and mind on a deeper level. You are reminding yourself that you deserve love and compassion by taking time out of your day for activities that promote relaxation and peace, such as meditation, exercise, or reading a book. Self-care can boost your immune system, reduce stress levels, enhance your moods, and allow personal development. There are numerous benefits to introducing self-care activities into our routine, which makes it all the more critical for us to prioritise them for our improvement and health.

Maintaining Self-Control

Self-control allows us to regulate our emotions, thought processes, and behavior. Practicing self-control can help us make better decisions that can lead toward achieving goals. It also can assist us in avoiding making rash decisions that could otherwise cause us to regret in hindsight. In addition, having self-control means looking objectively at a situation before coming up with an appropriate response rather than letting emotions dominate the way we think and behave. To build our self-control, we need practice and consistency in increasing our ability to monitor our thoughts, pick up on environmental cues, and regulate our reactions to challenging situations.

A. Creating New Habits

Crafting new habits is crucial for becoming a better version of ourselves, and maintaining self-control is one of the key elements needed to make this happen. The first step in acquiring more self-control is to recognise what needs to be changed. Consider your goals and how much effort it will take to break old patterns that no longer serve you. It's also vital to accept that challenges are going to arise. However, commitment and consistency make limiting personal impulses easier over time. Each day we must choose whether our focus will be on short-term pleasure or long-term rewards. Whatever decision is made should reflect what deserves priority in life.

B. Practicing Mindfulness

Practicing mindfulness is critical to gaining and maintaining self-control. Through mindfulness, one can improve conscious awareness of thoughts and feelings to break the cycle of impulsive behavior. Self-control means thinking through choices before making a decision, ultimately leading to better long-term decisions. Mindfulness is not only helpful in managing difficult emotions but also helps develop attitude transformation. By creating skills that allow us to utilise mindful awareness, we can remain aware of our emotional triggers and make conscious choices regarding how we respond to our environment. With mindfulness practice, one can increase their ability to stay composed even in stressful situations and maintain a sense of peace throughout chaotic events.

C. Identifying Triggers

It is essential to identify triggers if you are serious about maintaining self-control. One can take several steps to recognise behaviors or situations that may be difficult for them and cause them to lose self-control. Firstly, it helps to notice patterns of behavior. When a pattern becomes observable, the person can take notes and make a conscious effort not to become overwhelmed in those circumstances. Additionally, by focusing on their feelings and identifying how they lead them to respond, they can start understanding what causes an uncomfortable reaction within themselves. Finally, evaluating these reactions regularly will help the individual build up coping skills, so they don't succumb to uncontrolled outbursts or behavior. Recognising triggers is critical to cultivating self-control and overall self-awareness.

D. Reframing Negative Thoughts

Negative thoughts have the power to ruin our lives, and we must learn to reframe them. The key to maintaining self-control and keeping negativity in check is to be mindful of our thoughts and how they affect us. We need to recognise these negative thoughts when they arise, observe them without reacting, question their validity, and devise productive ways of addressing them. Rather than letting these thoughts control us, we can use proven techniques such as visualisation, self-affirmations, gratitude, or deep breathing exercises to manage our emotions in difficult situations. Reframing negative thoughts is a lifelong practice, but our thought process can improve drastically with consistency and patience.

E. Handling Relapses

It can be challenging to maintain self-control when facing a relapse. Remember that it's just a momentary setback and that you must take the necessary steps to recover quickly and get back on track. Finding healthy distractions can help relieve some of the stress of relapsing. Try exercising or spending time doing something enjoyable with family or friends. Practicing mindfulness techniques such as deep breathing or meditation for even a few minutes each day is beneficial to help calm your mind and reset your focus. Having a solid support system is vital. Reach out to someone if you need help maintaining self-control during relapse. Through proper care, self-love, and having an effective strategy in place, you'll return on course without letting the setback become permanent.

Key Takeaways

- Improving conscious awareness of thoughts and feelings can help break the cycle of impulsive behaviors.

- Identifying triggers is an essential part of developing self-control.

- Reframing negative thoughts is necessary for maintaining emotional control and reducing stress.

- Having a solid support system is essential when facing a relapse.

- Practicing mindfulness techniques such as deep breathing and meditation can help reset focus and emotions.

Action Step

Check-in with yourself regularly to evaluate how you're feeling and why. Take note of patterns in your behavior and identify triggers that may cause a loss of self-control. Develop an action plan for moments of relapse, such as engaging in healthy activities or calling on a trusted confidant to help manage emotions.

Chapter Summary

Self-control is an essential component of living a healthy, productive life. One can cultivate self-control skills by understanding the importance of having a solid support system, engaging in self-care, and developing strategies to identify triggers, reframe negative thoughts, and handle relapses, which will prove invaluable in all aspects of life. With mindful awareness and consistent practice, self-control can be achieved with time and dedication. With the proper techniques and a positive attitude, one can become more in control of themselves and the results that come from it. The journey to self-control is rewarding and worth the effort. With it, a person can lead a more fulfilling life with greater peace of mind!

CONCLUSION

Self-discipline is critical to turning our dreams into reality. By committing ourselves to make small changes along the way, we can slowly but surely reach our goals and achieve far more than we ever imagined. Self-discipline equips us with the tools to set measurable objectives and monitor our progress. It also allows us to stay focused on our end goals, no matter how difficult things get in the short term. As successful people often say, consistency and hard work set us apart.

When it comes to improving ourselves, and our lives, the path of self-discipline is one of the most rewarding and successful routes we can take. Working on self-discipline gives us the strength to endure any journey in life. It unleashes our inner potential and allows us to go after what we truly desire. It is also essential to understand that this journey will be challenging and require patience and perseverance to reap the rewards. We need to trust our inner voice and listen carefully to make progress. Embracing self-discipline within ourselves can sometimes feel like a challenge, but it ultimately makes us more fulfilled.

Throughout this guide, we have acquired valuable lessons that supply us with the knowledge base necessary to reach our aspirations. Whether it's acing college exams or building a business empire, these concepts provide the critical skills we need to be successful. Taking what we've learned and utilising it in dedication to our goals allows us to set off on a journey of self-fulfillment, one in which our ambition can finally reach its desired outcome. It's only when equipped with a solid understanding of the fundamentals that anything is indeed possible.

The idea of self-discipline requires effort to make it a part of our lives. But this effort pales compared to the benefits one can realise if one follows through and stays on a path of self-discipline. With every step taken, whether small or large, on this journey to true self-discipline, a new level of mental strength, resilience, and focus can be achieved. The key is staying consistent, making it part of our life's routine, and celebrating the results as we move along. With these principles in mind, it's time to apply the lessons from this guide in our daily lives!

REFERENCES

Amadi, A. (2022, May 23). Seven simple habits to improve your self-discipline. Clever Girl Finance.
https://www.clevergirlfinance.com/blog/7-simple-habits-to-improve-your-self-discipline/

Gleeson, B. (2020, August 25). 9 powerful ways to cultivate extreme self-discipline. Forbes.
https://www.forbes.com/sites/brentgleeson/2020/08/25/8-powerful-ways-to-cultivate-extreme-self-discipline/

Kennedy, T. (2008, March 12). How to build self-discipline to excel in life. Lifehack.
https://www.lifehack.org/articles/productivity/self-discipline-the-foundation-of-productive-living.html

Manson, M. (2019, February 8). If self-discipline feels difficult, then you're doing it wrong. Mark Manson.
https://markmanson.net/self-discipline

MindTools. (n.d.). Mindtools.com.
https://www.mindtools.com/adjf7nz/self-discipline

Prater, M. (2018, July 6). Secrets of self-discipline: How to become supremely focused. HubSpot.
https://blog.hubspot.com/sales/self-discipline

Self-discipline: Definition, tips, & how to develop it. (n.d.). The Berkeley Well-Being Institute.
https://www.berkeleywellbeing.com/self-discipline.html

Made in United States
Orlando, FL
16 June 2023